Strategy Manual

How to build relevant competitive advantage

Bas van Heel

Uitgeverij Helium

2018

Strategy Manual

How to build relevant competitive advantage

Author:	Bas van Heel
Illustrations:	iStock, CartoonStock
Proofreading:	Proof-Reading-Service.com, UK
Graphic Design:	Helium, grafische vormgeving
Publisher:	Uitgeverij Helium, NL

ISBN: 978-90-79841-10-3
NUR: 801

Keywords: management, strategy, customer needs, competitive advantage, manual, checklist, examples

This is not a work of fiction, but I have simplified and dressed up the examples for the sake of clarity.

Available from Amazon.

info@uitgeverijhelium.nl

Uitgeverij Helium

Executive summary ⇨

Do you understand your customer's needs?

"Waiter, there's no fly in my soup."

Do you understand your sources of competitive advantage?

"Hey, that's not fair!"

Are these sources of competitive advantage relevant?

Do you understand relevant competitive advantage before you build a business model?

"I don't get it. . . . Our business model was exactly the same."

The core of any strategy is an iterative approach to build relevant competitive advantage:

Relevant competitive advantage

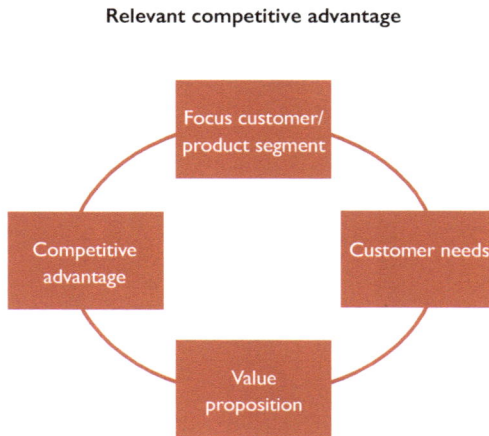

The complete (ten element) strategy is not rocket science, just (hard) work and creativity:

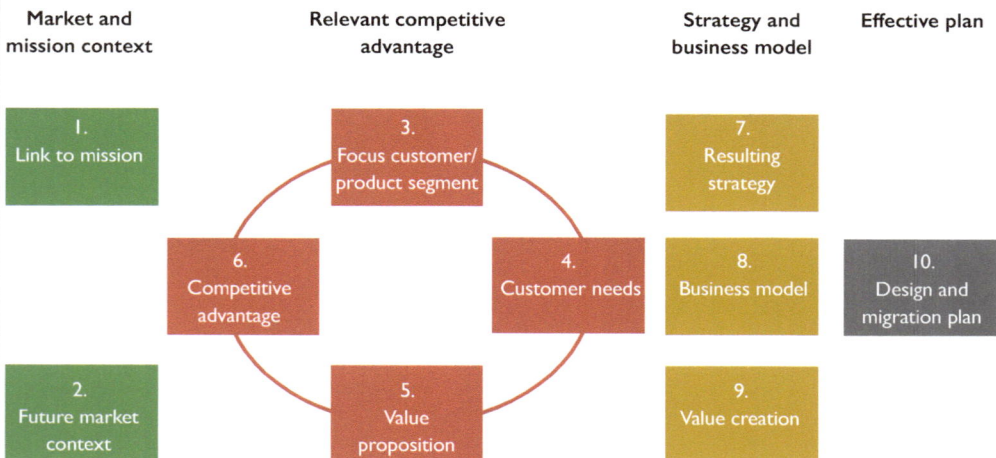

Contents

A Introduction: the objective of this manual

In 2017, I was a mentor for two Executive MBA (EMBA) students who were doing their in-company project. They asked for my help to apply the various conceptual frameworks that they had learned about, and which book they could use. However, I could not find what they needed, so I wrote this short manual instead. Later, I checked with a full EMBA class: most of them, indeed, wanted to learn how to apply the theory. So this book is not about new thinking on strategy but instead aims to apply the various concepts (elements) of strategy in a coherent way. It is a manual and check-list for people with years of experience in their company or function but who are relatively new to being involved in (part of) a company-wide strategy process.

When using a draft of this manuscript in an EMBA class, a third of the participants said that this was all common sense (this made me very happy!). After actually applying a checklist based on this approach, plus one in-depth exercise, just two participants still thought that it was common sense. So I hope you will not (just) read this manual for inspiration (who reads manuals for inspiration?) but will actually use it to assess or build your strategy.

The core of the book is about customer needs and competitive advantage. I have seen EMBA courses and training schemes for start-ups that either focus on competitive advantage or on customer needs. To me, the essence of strategy is to link both sides. Although it sounds obvious and simple, it is not often applied (properly).

B Example case

I found myself at a barbecue in the middle of nowhere in the US. It was warm, I knew nobody, and I felt a little bit lost in the vast space of the various assembly halls. But the hosts were very friendly and they were happy to show me around. They also provided me with ample food and drinks. The event was an open day at a flight simulator manufacturing company.

I was wondering what I was doing here. I was looking into the market for flight simulators as my second project for a consulting company. A technology company and a university had asked us if or how they should jointly enter the market for flight simulators. The technology company had already sold simulators for trains, and the university had sufficient experience in modelling and simulating an aerodynamic problem that was causing some planes to crash. This venture seemed to be a good idea but they realised they did not understand the market.

So I made a plan for understanding the market size, growth, customer needs and competitive situation. In those days, we did not have the Internet but we had a fantastic 'knowledge expert' who found a database with all of the flight simulators ever sold, including producer, operator, and so on. So that was the first part of the project done in a day's work and I had a lot of time to travel around the world to interview the test/training pilots of all the main airlines to understand the customers' needs. Studying the competition was quite simple: there were only three suppliers. And the customers were happy to talk about them. To complete the picture, I also asked to talk to all three suppliers but was only invited by the third supplier. The smallest supplier had smartly focused on a 'tail' segment that the two big players had ignored. This segment was actually not so small and it was growing fast. They even invited me to their open day with a luxury barbecue. I had written to them in advance to tell them that I was working for a potential competitor, but they still showed me around the various simulators being assembled and they told me about their new ideas. Not much later, I understood why they were self-confident enough to invite a potential future competitor.

We eventually advised against entering this market selling flight simulators. The alternatives for entering were to buy Player 3 or to sell expertise to the three flight simulator companies. Our clients were happy with the clear market analysis but not with the corresponding conclusion. We made it easier for them to accept the conclusions by changing the perspective from inside-out to outside-in:

Original inside-out view (simplified)

Competitive advantage
We sell simulators for trains
We have global distribution
We have a large technology base
We have cash
Good model for specific aerodynamic problem
Continuous research on flight (simulator) aerodynamics

Outside-in view (simplified): *(H=High, M=Middle, L=Low)*

Customers' needs	Priority of need	Score competitor 1	Score competitor 2	Score competitor 3	Score client company	Source of competitive (dis)advantage
Uptime	1	H	H	H	-	Cumulative learning on all simulators/by type
Availability of local specialist service	2	H	H	H	-	Regional share
Quality of visuals	3	M	L	H	-	Access to new visual technologies
Quality of updates	4	H	H	H	-	Share by type and learning capabilities
Experience with aircraft manufacturer	5	H	H	H	-	Share by manufacturer
Aerodynamic similarity vs real aircraft	6	M	M	M	H for one issue	Access to aerodynamic modelling

In summary, the supply side was completely consolidated into three players, where Players 1 and 2 focused on the segment of larger aircraft, and Player 3 focused on the smaller aircraft segment. The two priority customers' needs were fully satisfied by the current suppliers and they were hard to match by a new player because the underlying competitive advantage for these needs was (cumulative) share. The fight was over customer need 3: new visual technologies offered the possibility of changing the visual from schematic to virtual reality, which is the biggest step towards a perfect simulation. However, our clients did not have access to this visual technology. Their technology was relevant, but only for a small element of a low customer priority. The conclusion was that they did not have a sufficient competitive advantage that was relevant for the critical customer needs.

Following the discussion with our clients about our findings, I read in the news that Warren Buffet had bought Player 3. I was pleased because this news confirmed my view that this company was in a good situation. It had a near monopoly in a fast growing specific segment, with high barriers to entry and access to the technology that was able to address the main missing customer need. I then understood why the company was self-confident enough to invite a potential new entrant to its barbecue.

C Context and scope

Market economy
This strategy manual assumes that you operate in a market economy, where the customers are free to buy what they want. Most economies have developed into some kind of market economy, with competition authorities more or less protecting choice and transparency. Although the digital revolution initially supported transparency and customer choice, digital platforms have recently become so strong that they have started to act as virtual monopolies, taking all the profit from a market segment. However, I still think that strategy needs to be based on the customer needs.

If you really are in a legal monopoly, then you can still use most of this manual. Ask yourself, who would be your toughest competitors if tomorrow your monopoly were to be lifted? Most companies would then see sufficient potential competitors to spark the creative process of improvement in the face of (imaginary) competition.

Static or dynamic strategy
Some people have asked me if the classic 'static' strategy is over because we all live in an ever-changing market and need to become agile rather than do 'static' strategy.

I agree that technology changes quickly and the lifetime of companies is falling. This just means that you need to check/update your strategy more frequently than the 'once every three year strategy review'. But the fundamentals of working on strategy as set out in this manual still apply.

Companies and profit as proxy for a wide range of organisations
I elaborate this strategy manual around companies and making profit but the approach is equally valid for other types of organisation and mission, as long as they have to compete: for example NGOs who are competing for funding and for a licence to operate in a country.

Scope
This manual is comprehensive with respect to building and executing a strategy, so the *Elements of a good strategy* (as listed in Chapter E) can be used as a check list. However, as mentioned in the introduction, this manual focuses on building sustainable relevant competitive advantage. Therefore, for some elements we only explain the element and we refrain from going deeper. This is the case for financing, organising and preparing for implementation.

D Levels of strategy (corporate, business, functional)

We can distinguish three levels of strategy:

Corporate strategy
- Mission definition
- Business portfolio
- Legal structure
- M&A
- Financing

Business strategy

Functional strategies
- Digital
- Innovation
- Sales and Marketing
- Operations
- Sourcing/supply chain
- Organisation

This manual focuses on business strategy, while some of the approaches can also be used for the other two levels of strategy, complemented by the following analysis:

- A corporate strategy also needs to be based on relevant competitive advantage, but usually at a higher aggregation level. For instance, the 'where to play' question is more about which industries to play in rather than which subsegment to play in. Additional analyses are required, such as industry attractiveness analyses.
- A functional strategy needs to be linked to the corporate and business strategy. Check the relevant competitive advantage to see where the functional strategy can add value to the strategy. But, obviously, many additional function-specific analyses are required.

A business strategy can be created in different contexts related to the business cycle, such as: start-up, market entry, adding adjacencies, acquisition, transformation, and restructuring, and exit. I will not spend much time distinguishing between these because the logic of this manual can be easily adapted to the phase of the business cycle, for example: for start-ups, some of the elements mentioned under corporate strategy (e.g. mission, financing) need to be incorporated, but the core is about customer needs/competitive advantage.

In addition, B2C, B2SME, and B2B, businesses are different. However, in any context the elements in this manual are relevant, even if the mix of importance will vary. Although selling nuclear power plants is different from a start-up in electric scooters, in both cases you need to worry about the customers' needs and your own competitive advantage.

Elements of a good strategy

In my experience, strategy is not much more than finding out what your customers want and delivering on that better than anyone else.
If we want to phrase this a bit more formally, then we can say: 'customer needs/competitive advantage'.
If we want to be more comprehensive, then we elaborate:

A strategy is: ... a plan

⇨ Yes, but to do what?
> *A plan **to build relevant sustainable competitive advantage**.*

⇨ But why?
> *An **effective** plan to build relevant sustainable competitive advantage **to achieve your mission**.*

⇨ But what is 'relevant'?
> *An effective plan to build sustainable competitive advantage **into your value proposition to serve key customer needs in your focus segments** to achieve your mission.*

⇨ How much does it help my mission?
> *An effective plan to build sustainable competitive advantage into your value proposition to serve key customer needs in your focus segments, **to create significant value**, which is aspired to in your mission.*

⇨ How do we build this?
> *An effective plan to build sustainable competitive advantage into your value proposition to serve key customer needs in your focus segments, to create significant value aspired to in your mission, **by adapting your business model**.*

We will take the last sentence as the basis for this book, but I suggest that you use a shorter version when talking about strategy.

Let us break down the last sentence and list each element in a logical order:

1. Link to mission
2. Sustainable versus future market context
3. Focus segment
4. Customer needs
5. Value proposition
6. Competitive advantage
7. Resulting strategy
8. Required business model
9. Value creation
10. An effective plan

Grouped into logical clusters, we get:

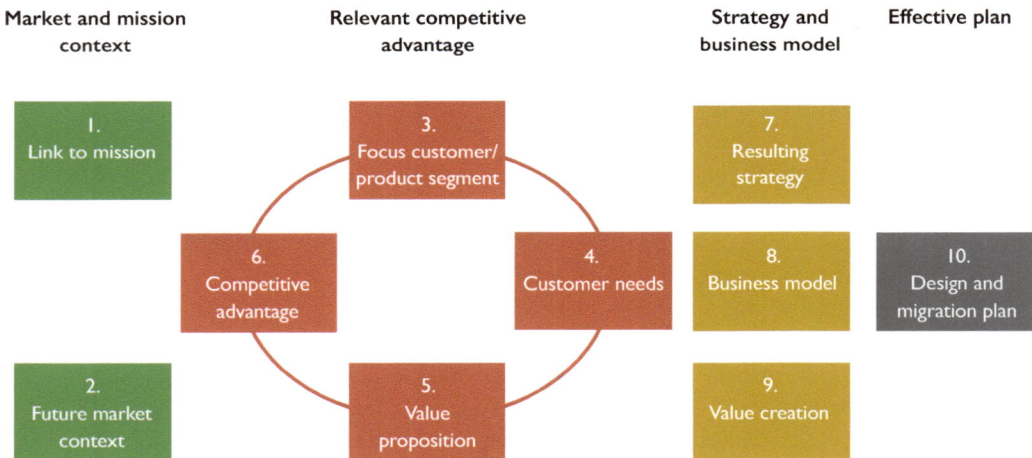

Market and mission context	Relevant competitive advantage	Strategy and business model	Effective plan
1. Link to mission	3. Focus customer/ product segment	7. Resulting strategy	
	6. Competitive advantage 4. Customer needs	8. Business model	10. Design and migration plan
2. Future market context	5. Value proposition	9. Value creation	

In early 2018, I asked an EMBA group of about 80, as an exercise, to assess a strategy they were close to (many took their company strategy) against these elements (based on this manuscript). About a third of each element was not done or was not done well enough (even in the four core red elements). Some were a result of not having full access to the strategies assessed, but many people told me that they had tried and failed to get the gaps filled. If three of the above elements are missing or badly done, then the resulting strategy is unlikely to be very good.

In my view, the four red steps are the heart of the strategy. Don't worry about where to start in these four steps: it is perfectly fine to have a great value proposition and then find a relevant customer segment. Or have a great new technology and then find a suitable customer segment/value proposition. Even people starting with their favourite target segment often switch to another segment because they find their competitive advantage can play out stronger there.

In principle, we work from left to right; however, strategy formation needs a highly iterative approach. In practice this means:

- Build the 'market and mission context'.
- Iterate within the four elements of 'relevant competitive advantage'.
- Check the 'relevant competitive advantage' against the 'market and mission context'.
- Build the 'strategy and business model' and iterate with the 'relevant competitive advantage'.
- Finalise the 'strategy and business model' and translate to 'design and migration plan'.

It may seem that this would take a lot of time but with the right conditions elements 1-9 could be done in 6-10 weeks for most businesses. More detail will be given in Chapter F: *How to run a strategy process*.

An overview of these ten elements, including the underlying factors:

Market and mission context
1. **Link to mission**
    1.1. Ensure that you have a good mission to drive your strategy
    1.2. Ensure the strategy will be the link between the mission and operational planning
    1.3. Choose an appropriate ambition level

2. **Future market context**
    2.1. Take a future perspective to avoid fighting the last war
    2.2. Understand the impact of trends
    2.3. Build options against scenarios to manage uncertainty

Relevant competitive advantage
3. **Focus product/customer segment**
    3.1. Creatively define customer segments based on common needs
    3.2. Define product segment and corresponding market/product segment matrix
    3.3. Determine market/product segment attractiveness

4. **Key customer needs**
    4.1. Define the customer Decision Making Unit, (incl. indirect DMU)
    4.2. Define and prioritise customer needs (incl. implicit/unmet)

5. **Value proposition**
    5.1. Creatively build the proposition
    5.2. Determine customer value (what it does for the customer)
    5.3. Link proposition to business model
    5.4. Define the product itself

6. **Competitive advantage**
    6.1. Define (potential) competitors
    6.2. Score your current and target performance versus competitors on customer needs
    6.3. List current and selected potential new sources of competitive advantage
    6.4. Understand the economics of sources of advantage
    6.5. Check (again) competitive advantage versus customer needs

Strategy and business model

7. Resulting strategy

    7.1. Decide where to play

    7.2. Summarise how to play

    7.3. Translate into a coherent strategy

    7.4. Incorporate stakeholders perspective

8. Required business model

    8.1. Map the required changes in business model

    8.2. Decide how to realise these changes

    8.3. Determine how to adjust the organisation and metrics

    8.4. Build the new culture into the new values, organisation, processes, and metrics

    8.5. Adapt the design to retain/enhance workforce engagement

    8.6. Take care of the enablers

    8.7. Ensure to cash in on the benefits

9. Value creation

    9.1. Include a base case

    9.2. Quantify the impact of the strategy

    9.3. Determine financing needs

    9.4. Conduct a risk analysis

Effective plan

10. Design and migration plan

    10.1. Adjust the team, add programme management, arrange the proper mandate

    10.2. Build a roadmap to sequence main changes

    10.3. Design processes and organisation and run pilots

    10.4. Design the migration

    10.5. Communicate and listen

    10.6. Check the change (process) management

    10.7. Build a people transition plan

    10.8. Design and build the implementation support team

1 Link to mission

1.1. Ensure that you have a good mission to drive your strategy

Working on strategy assumes that you have a good mission. A mission statement needs to be short, simple, clear, memorable, and long term. But most importantly, it needs to discriminate between strategies that will or will not contribute to achieving the mission.

These are a few examples that I like:

- Original Microsoft (1970s): *'A computer on every desk and in every home'*
- Original Ford (1900s): *'Democratize the automobile'*
- Nike (1960s): *'Crush Adidas'* (this is clear, but focuses on a competitor, not on customers, not ideal)
- Komatsu (1960s): *'Encircle Caterpiller'* (Komatso was a new entrant into the US bulldozer market and entered in niche segments, and encircled caterpillar), (https://en.wikipedia.org/wiki/Komatsu_Limited)
- Google (current): *'Organize the world's information and make it universally accessible and useful'*

The ones that I don't like are often too long. I don't want to offend anyone, so I will not show a list of bad ones. If you want to read more, just check out the Internet: it is full of examples of good and bad mission statements. More importantly, check out your own company's mission statement and see if it works. If you are not happy with the mission statement, then realise that building one is, in itself, a kind of strategy project, albeit at a higher abstraction level.

Some readers may comment that I fail to distinguish between a vision and a mission statement. The reason is that they are too similar.

1.2. Ensure that the strategy will be a link between the mission and operational planning

A mission, a strategy, and an operational plan (budget) have different functions and need to be kept apart.

Type of plan:	Mission →	Strategy →	Operational
Horizon (year)	5-20	3-5	1-3
Frequency (year)	> 10	1-3	1
Output-detail	one line	one PP /word doc	Target tree

Corporate

Business — This manual

Functional

The strategy needs to support the mission and the operation plan needs to be a translation of the strategy. In contrast, as I learnt from one of my clients, avoid tight coupling between the three levels of planning process because this reduces the freedom to think outside the box and risks getting stuck in details at the strategy and mission level. Tight coupling needs to exist on strategic choices, but not so much on all the metrics.

Sometimes, the operational strategies have longer timelines than the business strategy, often in the IT/digital realm. In these cases, the operational strategy either needs to be incorporated into the business strategy as a constraint or an IT/digital turnaround/transformation is required.

1.3.   Choose an appropriate ambition level

I was talking with someone who was working in a company with a unique position. They were selling into a $50bn market growing at 5% a year, consuming about $5bn of supplies. They had $50m revenues, representing a 50% share in their current product range. The leading brand was selling supplies into this market segment (at 1% market share in this broader definition).

What should be their ambition?

- Maintain current growth at 5% a year (i.e. grow with the market)
- Double the growth by increasing share to secure their position in their core offering
- Double the growth by adding adjacencies
- Consolidate the suppliers into this market

Strategically, all options seemed feasible (but the resulting roadmap/financing/ organisation would look very different). The answer depended more on the appetite of shareholders and management. Later, a new CEO appeared and one of the higher ambition levels was chosen.

2 Future market context

2.1. Take a future perspective to avoid fighting the last war

Realise that operationalising the strategy will take some time and that the required impact will take even more time. Therefore, we need to build strategy against the future market context to avoid 'fighting the last war'. So, make sure to look ahead, rather than backwards. For all elements of the strategy, use the same forward-looking time horizon as the strategy:

- Describe the market and its segments.
- Competitors: include your best estimate on their moves on the timeline over which you will be building and executing your strategy.
- Market: (mega)trends and technologies: quickly select critical ones, and work on the implications.
- Business cycle: your strategy horizon may put you in a different part of the business cycle than where you are at today.
- Financial forecasting: I have seen many companies translating their growth plan into an additional Ebit % increase due to scale advantages, forgetting that in a competitive market the scale advantage that you and your competitors receive will erode towards the customer. Similarly, some online stores think that once they have good penetration, their acquisition cost will reduce and repeat customer economics will improve profitability. The problem is that this only works if we are the only online store in a chosen segment.

2.2. Understand the impact of trends

This is more than a mind-set but it is an explicit piece of work. List all of the trends that may affect your relevant competitive advantage. This is the easy part but it adds no insight. Translate these trends into the impact on market/segment size, your customer's issues/needs and your competitive position. This impact analysis is valuable because it can turn up unforeseen opportunities and threats. Spend some real time on this.

2.3. Build options against scenarios to manage uncertainty

If uncertainties are too large and more effort will not bring more certainty, then create scenarios and options and translate these into minimum viable actions or a bold choice. Realise that this is quite some extra work, so only do this for serious structural uncertainties.

People often confuse scenarios and options:
*   A scenario is a coherent set of market/context changes. You can (and often should) try to influence the market context such that the scenario that works best for you happens, but the essence of the scenario concept is that you will not be sure which one will really materialise.
*   An option is a cause of action on your part.

Options	Scenario 1 Market shrinks 10% a year	Scenario 2 Market is liberalised	Scenario 3 Both
O1. Raise prices	x		
O2. Improve products		x	x
O3. Hard cost reduction			x
O4. No regret actions	x	x	x

For each scenario you will build a relevant strategy option and a set of activities useful under any scenario (called the no-regret actions).
Obviously these options will be built in subsequent steps but the decision to work in options versus scenarios needs to be made early on, when the impact of key trends is very uncertain.

The more entrepreneurial company will then make a bold choice and gamble on one scenario, and invest in the best option for that scenario so that they are best positioned when the scenario materialises.
The more conservative company will invest in the no-regret options (aspects that benefit all options under any scenario), and really invest in the best option once it is clear which scenario will materialise.
A good in-between approach is to find the rate determining steps for each option (such as hiring a few critical people or getting a license on a critical technology) and then invest in those. This way, the lead time to jump onto such options is reduced. When combined with a good active watch on the changing market context, you may become the most adaptive company.

3. Focus product/market segment

We need to define the product/market segmentation to map out the options where we want to enter (start-up) or where to add adjacencies or grow our competitive advantage (existing player in many segments). In practice, this is done from the top down, making a product market matrix and refining this along the way.
Let us explore the customer and product dimension separately.

3.1. Creatively define market segments based on common needs

Only monopolists (think they) don't need to worry about segmentation. This is often what kills them in the end because they will have a one size fits all solution for all different/changing customer needs. Ordinary companies already know they need to worry about which segments to play in because they cannot afford to be the best in all segments.

This segmentation serves a different purpose, depending on what kind of company you are:
- As a start-up, you may want to start in one segment and later work your way into adjacent segments.
- As an established player in a small number of segments, you may want to choose between growing in your current segments and/or adding another.
- As an established player, present in many/all segments, you may want to improve profitable growth by investing in a selection of your segments. In any case you need to segment the market.

A market segment is defined as a group of customers that have the same needs. This segmentation can be done by applying classical segmentation dimensions:
- Geography: global, regional, national, local
- Customer size: corporate, SME, retail
- Industry (sub)sector
- Retail: income, age

But you can be more creative: (hard to be generically creative here, depends on your business)
- Industry leaders, versus followers/laggards
- Early adopters, early/late followers
- High growth customers
- Users where my service/product determines a large part of their success

- Value buyers versus price buyers
- Product versus full service buyers
- First time versus repeat buyers

And then you can be even more creative, based on an iteration with your 'competitive advantage' and 'proposition' as per the subsequent chapters. Sometimes a brilliant strategy is based on choosing a focus segment in a very creative way. Given that digital marketing makes it easier to find your segment, we can afford to be more creative. In the past, a T-shirt maker producing a very special T-shirt specifically for people who sweat a lot would have found it difficult to stock their product in all the stores. Today, in the context of an online store, they can find customers much more easily and can sell their product online only.

3.2. Define the product segment and the corresponding market/product segment matrix

Some people get carried away and slip product elements into the customer segmentation — don't!
You can find the product options by either exploring what the customer segments (could) use/buy or by extending your existing product range.
In the imaginary example of the shirt maker who started to make T-shirts for people who sweat a lot, let us assume that he defined his mission as: "I dress people with unusual needs" (a fully online proposition, products that fashion stores refuse to stock).
His product market option matrix could look like:

	Men who sweat in EU	Men who sweat globally - EU	Women who sweat globally	Very tall / short people	Other unusual people (tbd)
T-shirts	Current position				
Underwear					
Shirts					
Trousers					
Rain jackets					

When he is properly established in the current segment, he probably needs to choose which segment to add next rather than to (ad)dress all at the same time. He may also want to choose to focus on a customer segment (the first two columns) or a product segment (e.g. the first row).

25

When iterating, avoid determining too many segments. Weed out the bad ones or cluster the good ones. Don't confuse products with product segments.

3.3. Determine market/product segment attractiveness

There are many ways to determine segment attractiveness:

- Size
- Growth
- Entry barriers
- Profit pools
- Business maturity
- Consolidation

Feel free to determine which one works for you, as long as you don't fall into the trap of adding the dimension of competitive advantage into segment attractiveness, which we want to show separately. In this manual, we use future profit pools as a proxy for segment attractiveness because this takes care of all the other factors. For 'future', use the same time horizon as the strategy planning horizon. For profit pools, make sure not to use your profit in that segment but do use the profit all suppliers make serving that segment. Don't get bogged down in trying to be very accurate, this is about profit pools being small or large, but do list the underlying drivers that are listed above because it helps with understanding the market:

- Determine the current market size in terms of revenues.
  Ideally build this up from a driver tree, starting with customers, because this will help in several other analyses. For instance, if you want to size the online market for prepared food: number of households X %households buying prepared food online X Frequency: orders per year X order size in dollars. Apply a sanity check by adding the revenues of all competitors.
- Apply five years of growth (if that is your strategy horizon) - the sizing driver tree will come in handy.
- Apply your peers' current average profitability.
- Determine if profitability will go down or up or remain stable (due to business cycle, change in barriers to entry, new entrants) and then apply this in order to derive the future profit pool.

A word of caution needs to be raised about prioritising premium/speciality segments. Many people think that profits are higher in the premium market (B2C) or specialities (B2B) segments. They confuse margin (surely they are higher) and profit (premiums/specialities cost more to produce and serve). The range of company profitability within the premium segment and within the commodity markets is usually much larger than the difference in profitability between the average premium and the average commodity player. Consequently, being the best within the premium or the commodity segment is more important than being in the premium segment, even for cyclical businesses. You can be profitable (over the cycle) even with a cyclical commodity, as long as you are much bigger and better then the next company.

4 Key customer needs

4.1. Define the customer DMU (including indirect DMU)

Find out who decides what and from whom to buy, this is the Decision Making Unit (DMU). This can be a single person but often it is a team (especially in B2B). The word DMU can be misleading because most decisions about suppliers are made by a range of people who do not act as a team (unit). Therefore, check if the classic roles in the DMU offer a new perspective: initiator, decider, buyer, Influencer, user, and gatekeeper.

4.2. Define and prioritise customer needs (including implicit/unmet needs)

Some people claim that it does not make sense to ask customers what they want because they don't know. I disagree, I think all strategy projects need to start with the customer to avoid you getting distracted by your own advantages/beliefs. How to do this depends on the level at which you want to understand the customer needs and how you go about finding out their needs.

"Waiter, there's no fly in my soup."

Explicit needs/buyer's level (for marketing, product adjustments)
This is the simplest level, the 'specs' at which the product is bought by the chosen customer segment. In some EMBA work, I have seen people list products as customer needs. That is not what we mean here. For example, for supermarket customers it is not: 'milk, bread, and sugar' but 'proximity, product range, and price'.

You can analyse this by:
- Surveying buying criteria
- Online: drop-off analysis
- Lost sales analysis
- NPS (Net Promoter Score)

Unmet/hidden/implicit needs level (for product development)
There are often implicit or unmet needs. Finding these provides an opportunity to build a better service/product ahead of the competition.

You can analyse this through:
- In-depth interviews, focus groups and surveys
- Quantitative surveys (e.g. conjoint analysis)
- Ethnography (study of how people use a product)
- Mapping the customer's journey and determining what the pain points are
- Mapping the customer's buying process
- Analysing in-use economics

For interviews and focus groups, the trick is not to ask about the needs you hope will emerge for your service product but to understand what people do, and translate this yourself to the unmet customer needs. (A good book to help you understand these interview techniques better is *The Mom Test*, by Rob Fitzpatrick.) Surveys can quantify these behaviours and they can then check some hidden needs.

System level (for segment prioritisation and R&D)
This approach is more suitable for determining new services/products than for tweaking existing ones.

You can analyse this by:
- Mapping the customer's industry value chain
- Analysing the customer's economics
- Analysing the customer's strategy and challenges

When mapping the customer needs, make sure to include all of the elements of the service/product and not just the product itself. Include the supply chain, customer service, recovery process and price. In short, include everything that is relevant for the complete customer journey. Although this may seem overdone for simple consumer products, most consumer products seem never to have been tested by consumers for non-core attributes (e.g. a pair of scissors packaged in hard plastic that can only be opened by a pair of scissors) and some seem not to have been tested for the core attributes either.

At the end, you may want to check and prioritise the customer needs list with a survey or more interviews to feel more secure to use it as the basis for the emerging strategy (and subsequent investments, communication, business model design).

After all that work, the result is a simple prioritised customer needs list that will determine where your (new) competitive advantages will be most effective.

5

Value proposition

5.1. Creatively build the proposition

Building a winning value proposition is a creative process. Many start-ups have started with a good idea/value proposition, not an analysis. This is perfectly fine, it does not really matter where the iteration starts in the core of the strategy (customer segment choice – customer needs – value proposition – competitive advantage).

If the thinking around customer needs and competitive advantage does not provide enough ideas, then apply some (obvious/less obvious) perspectives to brainstorm around:

- The mission: "What would it look like if . . ", the headline in 2025.
- BHAGS: https://en.wikipedia.org/wiki/Big_Hairy_Audacious_Goal
- The most impactful trends: reason through the implications for risks and opportunities.
- Destroy your own business: Understand (or start) new disruptive/deconstruction business models.
- Blue ocean strategies (propositions in segments without competition).
- Breaking compromises (e.g. individualised cars against mass market cost).
- Partnerships: What companies do you admire, what would yours bring to a partnership?
- Stranded assets: Because they are free, what can we do? (And then think about how to get more value rather than giving it away).
- New business models (see great list of examples in https://en.wikipedia.org/wiki/Business_model): How can they enhance the delivery of your competitive advantage? (Be careful to only use this for creativity, don't get sucked into building the business model before nailing down the relevant competitive advantage.)

When still working to find out the segment in which to play, you should distinguish value propositions at both the segment level and at individual product service level. By all means, note value propositions for specific products services for later product development but when still doing the strategy project avoid getting trapped into a detailed product development process before having determined the strategy at the segment level. For start-ups, the strategy and product development process may be less distinguishable for a while.

5.2.   Determine customer value (what it does for the customer)

A value proposition (for a product or service) needs to be defined in terms of what it does for a customer, but not in terms what you do to produce it.
If we follow the hypothetical T-shirt maker, then we need to think about what it does for our customers: the T-shirt reduces sweating, and when you sweat it evaporates better and stops the bacteria from developing a bad odour.
Now that we know what it does, we need to translate it into customer value.
In the shirt example: for 50% of the days, I don't have to change my T-shirt during the day, saving 10 minutes of hassle, $100s of laundry costs, and $100s of shirt life. We may not sell it in these $ terms, but quantifying helps to understand how a customer might appreciate the product.

5.3.   Link proposition to business model

Start iterating with the business model in mind (See chapter 8).
Manage between two traps:

*   Don't get sucked into quickly building a business model before you have properly understood your relevant competitive advantage.
*   Don't wait until you have found the perfect relevant competitive advantage and then find out that you cannot build it.
    Ideally, build a high-level version of the business model (the one pager) and use that to iterate the relevant competitive advantage until that is stable, and then start detailing the business model.

"I don't get it. ... Our business model was exactly the same."

5.4.　Define the product itself

Of course we also need to worry about the product. We need to be able to actually produce it. At this stage, we need to worry about it as far as a check if we will be able to deliver on the customer needs, not about the details.
In the example, the T-shirt is made from bamboo, produced in an environmentally sustainable way. The T-shirt maker has studied many designs, and has arrived at a small number of designs that incorporate all of the good design elements.

6 Competitive advantage

6.1. Define (potential) competitors

If we want to design how to better deliver on customer needs than our competitors, then we need to understand who our competitors are. A good way to find all the relevant competitors, is to apply *Porter's five forces* model (https://en.wikipedia.org/wiki/Porter's_five_forces_analysis). This model describes what types of company can act as competitors, and as such, erode our profit (profit as a proxy for the value we create for our customers):

- Industry rivalry: companies doing sort of the same as we do.
- New entrants: if profitability is high, then new players can enter.
- Suppliers: can squeeze our advantage if they become too powerful, or even shift their value proposition into ours.
- Customers: customer concentration can erode our profit, or they can even integrate backward into our proposition.
- Substitutes: if your proposition can be replaced by a better one, then you may be confronted with players from a completely different area. For example, if you run a taxi company, you may worry about other taxi companies, or Uber, but you probably need to worry more about the driverless car.

Be creative in applying this model to avoid missing important potential competitors. The result needs to be a list of competitors that you need to worry about most. Some people say that competitor analysis distracts from focussing on the customer.
I agree that in day-to-day work, most energy needs to be spent on finding ways to satisfy the customers but, every now and then, you need to calibrate your strategy to ensure that you are/will remain ahead of the game in your chosen segment.

6.2. Score your current and target performance versus the competitors on customer needs

Take the customer needs list as defined in Chapter 5.3, and score how you perform today on those needs. Add the list of competitors and do the same. Be brutally honest, and check it by having your customers do the scoring. Then add which customer needs you want to improve on.

Our T-shirt maker:

First, his current position in the EU, where he is well ahead of the competition.

Customer need	Priority of need	Score competitor 1	Score competitor 2	Score own company
Sweat less	1	L	L	H
Low smell	2	L	L	H
Good fit	3	M	L	H
Easy to buy	4	H	H	H
Low price	5	H	H	M
Overall score relevant competitive advantage for this segment				Very High

The situation below is if he were to enter non-EU areas, where he does not have the best type of materials, design or distribution.

Customer need	Priority of need	Score competitor 1	Score competitor 2	Score own company (current)	Score own company (new)
Sweat less	1	L	L	M	H
Low smell	2	L	L	M	H
Good fit	3	M	L	M	H
Easy to buy	4	H	H	L	H
Low price	5	H	H	M	M
Overall score relevant competitive advantage for this segment				Medium	High

6.3. List current and selected potential new sources of competitive advantage

"Hey, that's not fair!"

There are several ways to map sources of advantage. The simplest is structural advantage (often simplified into 'share' or scale) and capabilities. However, this is so important that I like to map them in a bit more detail by splitting the capabilities into: processes; people; culture and organisation; products, IP, technology and critical assets; digital and IT; and capital.

Share
High market share often provides a scale-driven cost advantage, depending on the type of business. For example, doubling the size of a container ship does not double the cost of the ship or operating it (if you can fill it). In contrast, plumbing services for residential areas only have a scale in marketing, so there is much more consolidation in container shipping than in plumbing services. The fight for dominant share/scale is an eternal struggle with the competition authorities if done by M&A. But if the proposition/competitive advantage is so strong that you can build an economic monopoly in a defendable segment on your own, then the competition authorities only have a limited influence.

The network is a special kind of scale. Networks connect sellers and buyers, or senders and receivers, and they benefit enormously from fragmentation at both sides. Once players have a high market share, then it is hard to enter, as DHL found when it entered the US in the duopoly (UPS and FedEx) express market: several billion dollars later, it had to pull out.

Processes
A bank found out that the percentage acceptance of its mortgage offers depended largely on the turnaround time. So it re-engineered its review process to be much faster. Some people think that improving processes makes them expensive, but usually the first and second round of re-engineering improves quality, costs and speed, before any compromises need to be made between costs and quality or speed.
On a more structural process-level, the invention of the air-hub and spoke model for express parcels gave FedEx an advantage for many years.

People
I once heard a CEO say that: "We make ordinary people do extraordinary things". This may work in a business with repetitive work, where the quality of the process design determines who is winning but in businesses with more complex processes, strong processes do not guarantee that you will win. You also need the best people in the areas that are critical in the eyes of the customer in your chosen segment.

Culture/organisation
Company culture is the set of behaviours prevalent in a company. They are often related to an original strategic focus. Strong cultures are so engrained into everyday habits and beliefs that they are hard to change. For example, one of the global express players has a very strong culture that is based on respect for the people in operations: even/especially in strategy meetings, no one should dress better than the drivers. It is a competitive advantage to always think about the primary process. Culture can also be an obstruction. For example, a company that was diversifying from being a monopoly player into a fully competitive world, had to actively redesign its culture from being risk-averse and process-driven to being entrepreneurial and customer-driven.

If a mortgage acceptance process is spread across several functions, and the CEO is the lowest person responsible for all required functions, then it is hard to compete on the fastest turnaround time (while still keeping the quality of the credit check). This problem can be resolved by creating a clear process with clear mandates across the functions, or by reorganising to have all relevant players on one team. Reorganisations are often initiated to resolve these sorts of issues. But often, one thing is resolved and several other problems are created. Meanwhile one or two years are wasted on focussing on the internal reorganisation instead of on the customers. 'Lean and Agile' can improve processes without having to reorganise and they can create tremendous competitive advantage on speed, quality and costs. However, sometimes reorganisation is necessary if the organisation is too misaligned with most of the critical processes to compete.

Products/IP/Technology/Critical assets
Some people claim that the source of all economic growth is technology. Since people started to specialise from being hunter-gatherers to farmers, the resulting scale advantage allowed people to invest in tools and processes to do whatever they focused on better. I think this is a good way to think about it.
Intellectual property can be defended by patents and/or by speed: getting to market quickly and taking a strong position.
Sometimes a company has critical assets: ideally ones that are combined with a technological advantage. For instance, shipping very large offshore installations requires very large and dedicated vessels. This results in very lumpy investments, which only the larger players can afford.

Digital capabilities
My first, and one of my last, projects as a consultant had a significant IT component: the IT legacy system problems were so complex that all strategic/tactical initiatives ran into IT trouble. New entrants with off-the-shelf IT platforms were eating into their markets. The digital revolution has made this issue significantly more critical because it allows new business models to take control. For those that get it right, speed up adaptations to market needs. Digital capabilities are much broader than IT capabilities. This is about understanding how the digital revolution will impact (threats and opportunities) your markets and business models. This situation often requires a digital/IT transformation.

Capital
Having a lot of capital (in cash or by being conservatively financed) can be an advantage. There are many ways to use this advantage: you can outbid competitors to buy start-ups with great complementary capabilities, customers and products. An offshore company recently found itself in the bottom of the cycle. It had more capital than its competitors, so it could play a game of chicken to wait until the weaker players had to give up, and it could then buy them or steal their customers. It could also afford to invest in new critical assets that would be ready when the cycle turned. Obviously, an overly conservative capital position can become a disadvantage: if you don't use it to create value, then your shareholders will want it back one way or another.

Advantage by part of the value chain
It is also important to understand what part of the value chain has the advantage of these sources of competitive advantage. This becomes even more important in a deconstructing market where you don't need to control all of the elements of a value chain to compete.
The business life cycle is another way to look at what part of the value chain to own. Some organisations are very good at creating new ideas, some are better at bringing them (first) to market, others are good at upscaling, and some are good at maturing or even managing down the end of the business cycle. Very few companies are good in all areas.

An interesting example is Rocket Internet, which is a successful incubator that replicates successful internet companies in countries where it has not been rolled out. They may not do the innovation, but are very good at replication and scaling up.

To show the full map (incorporating both the scale and detailed capabilities, as well as the main elements of the value chain), I selected an integrator model as an example. Below is an outside-in view on a global integrator express player. Grossly simplified: this company has many advantages in operations but given that the market context is becoming much more susceptible to last-mile robotisation (the autonomous vehicle), it would probably be good for them to invest in last mile technology and a more agile innovation process.

Source of competitive advantage by type and part in value chain Example: for a global Express player							Impact		
	Share/Scale	Process	People	Culture/ Organisation	Products/IP/ Technology/ Critical assets	Digital /IT	Capital	Quality	Low cost	Speed
Innovation/ R&D	H	M→H	M→H	M→H	M→H	M→H				M→H
M&A, alliances	H						H			
Marketing	H									
Sales & channels	H						H			
Customer service	H	H						H		H
Sourcing	H									
Production	H	H	H	H	L→H	H		H	L→H	H
Distribution										

I realise that there is an overlap between this overview of sources of competitive advantage and the value chain and activities list in the business model in subsequent sections. The reason for this set-up is that it means that we can check sources of competitive advantage without getting sucked into developing the details of a business model without the understanding of customer needs and competitive advantage.

Competitor intelligence

During a recent EMBA session someone mentioned that it was unusual to be able to get information directly from competitors, as described in the example in Chapter B. However, in the example most information about competitors came from interviewing the customers. The invitation to the company barbecue was nice but not vital. In practice, gathering information about the competitive situation requires similar creativity as understanding the customer needs.

A few suggestions to gather competitor intelligence (CI):

Determine what is critical information based on the source of competitive advantage map (don't simply collect what is easily available):
- If you want to grow by M&A, then make a long list with high level data, make short list with acquisition economics, logic, and playbook, and update regularly.
- If you are fighting segment by segment, with a small number of players, make a segment share database.
- If the competition is about costs, then make a competitor cost model (not the same as a pricing overview).
- If the competition is about first to market/first to critical share, then make a share database.
- If recruiting is a big part of winning, then collect info on offers; or even segment of one; analyse all cross/lost offers.

Design a process for regular analysis, the frequency should be based on needs/rate of change (not ad hoc).

Comply with the law and ethics: mostly two things:
- Comply with all applicable laws, both domestic and international.
- Accurately disclose all relevant information, including one's identity and organisation, prior to all interviews (this applies equally, whether the people gathering the information are staff or 3rd party representatives).

Be creative to gather CI: see table (but check what you need first)
- Customers, interviews, desk research, databases, modelling, online data analysis, field work, patents, and applicants.

Type of source	Source of competitor intelligence
Customers	Interview/survey on comp. performance on customer needs
Interviews	Industry experts (via expert networks such as GLG) Ex-employees People in your company with a good network Conferences
Desk research	Website (company and product data etc) Annual report Press, incl. product launches Publications (banks, sector organisations, etc)
Databases	Public (government) data sources Regulatory agencies Commercial data bases e.g. LexisNexis, Nielsen
Modelling	Cost model (use your own and adjust parameters) Segment share database
Online data analysis	Social media App statistics Search engine data & analytics
Field work	Google Earth (e.g. to size manufacturing sites) Store checks Test & Reverse engineer products
Patents	Patent technology and application analysis
Applicants	Analyse won and lost cross offers

6.4.   Understand the economics of the sources of advantage

Because price is often an important element of customer needs, you need to understand the economics of your (dis)advantages. The most basic one is the scale curve. A paper distribution company was targeting an increase in its market share in Europe, but saw its profitability decrease as a result. Paper distribution is largely a multi-local business. The company was gaining share by entering new markets or growing in low share countries, while it would be better to increase its share in countries where it could achieve a leading share.

Don't forget the scale curves' sister — the learning curve. They are not identical twins. The learning curve describes the percentage cost reduction for every cumulative doubling of the produced products without increasing the scale of the operation, because it continuously learns how to do things better. This is an important element of first mover advantage.

More broadly, it is important to quantify the source of competitive advantage for each of the customer needs (not just costs). If the bank halves its turnaround time for responding to a mortgage, then what increase in acceptance does that lead to?

6.5.   Check (again) competitive advantage versus customer needs

This is the real sanity check. Does my (quantified) source of competitive advantage improve an attribute that our customers actually care about? And will it make them stick with me or switch to me? Summarise all the work into something like the table in Chapter B (the outside-in view). Or better still, include the steps you like to take to improve on the competitive advantage, as in the example for our T-shirt maker.

Example: T-shirt maker: customer needs (new) competitive advantage for the segment: T-shirts for sweaty men outside the EU (globally)

Customer need	Priority of need	Score competitor 1	Score competitor 2	Score own company (current)	Source of competitive advantage (current)	Score own company (new)	Source of competitive advantage (additional)
Sweat less	1	L	L	M	Using special type of bamboo, deep ties with plantation. Not applicable to all climates.	H	Tested in various climates. Bamboo technology adjusted, and some countries deprioritised
Low smell	2	L	L	M	Using special type of bamboo, deep ties with plantation. Not applicable to all people.	H	Tested in various climates. Bamboo technology adjusted, and some countries deprioritised
Good fit	3	M	L	M	In depth study of 100s of designs. Own design and manufacturing. Not applicable to all people.	H	In depth study of 100s of designs, redone in new target countries
Easy to buy	4	H	H	L	100% online to repeat buyers. No supply chain/ existing customer base	H	Build supply chain, and invest in new customer acquisition
Low price	5	H	H	M	Small # sku's, manufacturing on low cost countries, simple short supply chain (no shops)	M	
Overall score				Medium		High	

At the end of the last chapter on relevant competitive advantage, I want to stress again the need for an iterative approach based on a few examples:

- The example in Chapter B (the example case) showed what happens if you focus too long on what you believe your competitive advantage is without checking (unmet) customer needs.

- A start-up team that I helped consisted of two designers who really mapped out the customer needs, chose a good subsegment to go deep into and designed a good value proposition in two months. The problem was there were already ample similar propositions in the market produced at scale. The better thought-through design could be easily copied by existing producers. So the team had to drive for an even more radical improvement on the unmet customer needs, looking for solutions that could turned into sustainable competitive advantage.

- I helped another start-up work through its proposition. It had a good idea about the customer needs but it had insufficient competitive advantage. So they improved the proposition but had to focus on a narrower segment. Eventually the segment size became too small to become financially attractive (could not pay the set-up costs). So a new iteration was needed.

The more often that you do a full iteration on all four aspects (the four 'red' elements: *Segment definition, Customer needs, Value proposition* and *Competitive advantage*), the faster you learn and avoid going too deep on one aspect, only to later find that it is a dead end. The art is knowing when to stop iterating and fix the customer segment and their needs, and then detail the value proposition and sources of competitive advantage.

7 Resulting strategy

7.1. Decide where to play

After the first few iterations in Chapters 3-6 on 'relevant competitive advantage', you should have ended up with a short list of these segments, including the future profit pools; for instance, along the lines of the nine segments in the example below. Note that although this T-shirt maker does exist, my strategic considerations are completely made up.

For each of these segments, summarise the future profit pool (in million dollars) and potential relevant competitive advantage:

	Men who sweat in EU	Men who sweat globally - EU	Women who sweat globally	Very tall / short people	Other unusual people (tbd)
T-shirts	27 / HH	177 / H	203 / H	Later	Later
Underwear	15 / H	79 / M	90 / M	Later	Later
Shirts	17 / L	71 / L	27 / LL	Later	Later
Trousers	Later	Later	Later	Later	Later
Rain jackets	Later	Later	Later	Later	Later

Later on, bamboo technology appeared not to be applicable and design simplification was not replicable to shirts. Consequently shirts were left out of the options. Also women were a difficult new segment, so four segment options remained for consideration.

Decision making for where to play can be further facilitated by mapping the segments into a matrix:

- X-axis: segment attractiveness in profit pools
- Y-axis: relevant competitive advantage as scored for each segment

In the following example, we have overlaid the actions that could be taken to increase the relevant competitive advantage.
This is not very different to a corporate portfolio's overview/options, but here it uses segments within a business rather than businesses within a corporation.

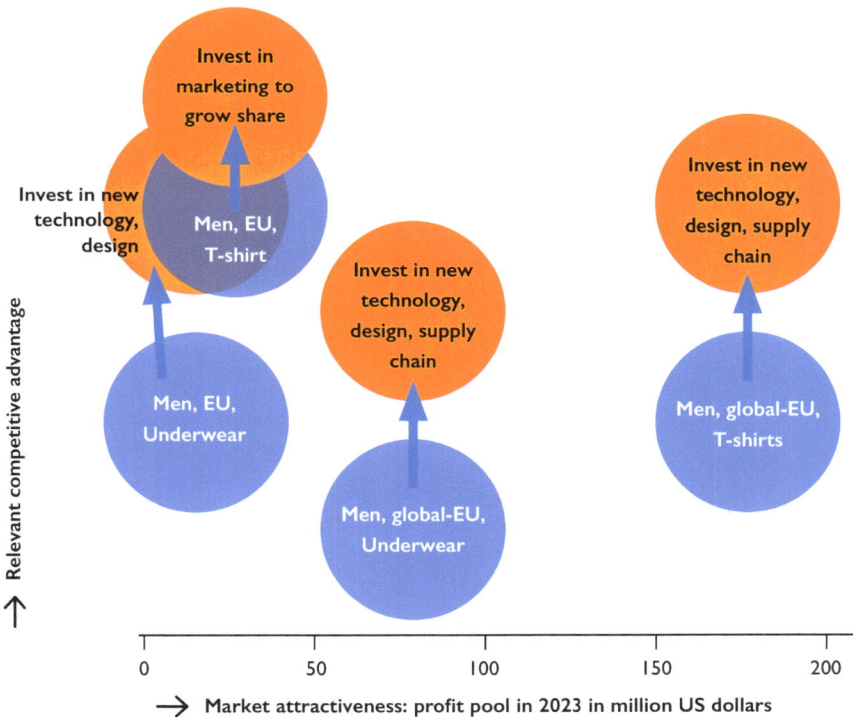

47

7.2.   Summarise how to play

First reiterate the sources of competitive advantage that you want to build (e.g.
to enter a new segment), see the example below. Focus on the right-hand column:
these are the new sources of competitive advantage to build. Although the example is a summary/simplified version, even if mapped a little more comprehensively,
such an overview can still look deceivingly simple. You really need to check the
degree to which existing positions are replicable elsewhere. It is easy to overlook
many different needs of country/customer segments, which can lead to the need
to make in costly adjustments once you have already entered this segment.

Example: T-shirt maker — (new) competitive advantage for the segment: T-shirts
for sweaty men outside the EU (globally)

Customer need	Source of competitive advantage (current)	Source of competitive advantage (additional)
Sweat less	Using special type of bamboo, deep ties with plantation. Not applicable to all climates.	Tested in various climates. Bamboo technology adjusted, and some countries deprioritised.
Low smell	Using special type of bamboo, deep ties with plantation. Not applicable to all people.	Tested in various climates. Bamboo technology adjusted, and some countries deprioritised.
Good fit	In depth study of 100s of designs. Own design and manufacturing. Not applicable to all people.	In depth study of 100s of designs, redone in new target countries.
Easy to buy	100% online to repeat buyers. No supply chain/existing customer base.	Build supply chain and invest in new customer acquisition.
Low price	Small number of stock keeping units, manufacturing on low cost countries, simple short supply chain (no shops).	

7.3.   Translate into coherent strategy

Translating the many adjustments for building relevant competitive advantage risks
becoming a shopping list of many things for many different customer segments.
Consequently, we need to find a way to describe and communicate a coherent
strategy. The risk of these generic strategies is choosing them early on and not
really understanding the relevant competitive advantage. If you truly understand
how to build relevant competitive advantage for your chosen segment's customer
needs, then don't worry too much about the strategy sticker on it. It is fine to call
it being the best in your chosen segment.

Most generic strategies are basically summaries of the map of sources of competitive advantage:

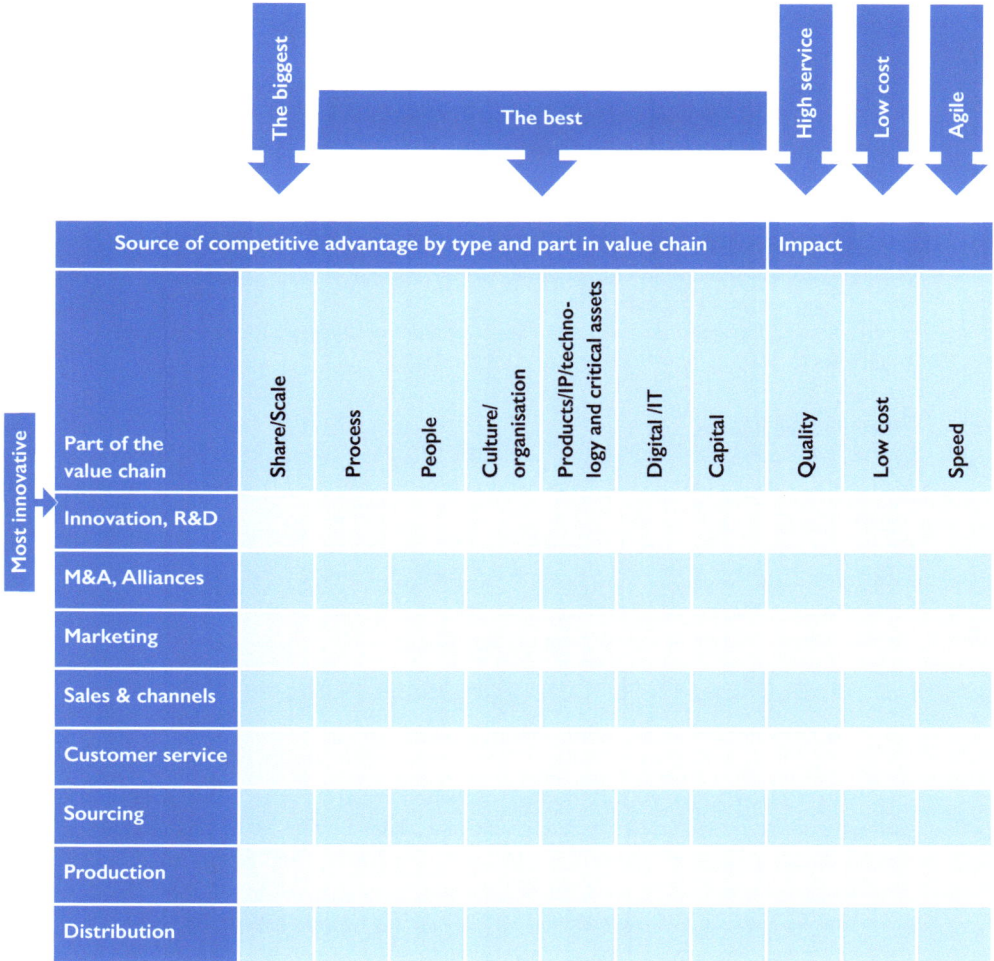

	The biggest	The best						High service	Low cost	Agile
Source of competitive advantage by type and part in value chain								**Impact**		
Part of the value chain	Share/Scale	Process	People	Culture/ organisation	Products/IP/techno- logy and critical assets	Digital /IT	Capital	Quality	Low cost	Speed
Innovation, R&D										
M&A, Alliances										
Marketing										
Sales & channels										
Customer service										
Sourcing										
Production										
Distribution										

Most innovative (vertical label on left side)

Being the largest

The assumption is that having the highest share in the chosen market segment yields the highest scale, not only in cost structure but also in resources to build the best processes and capabilities.

If you take this a bit further to building a virtual monopoly: if your M&A is completed before your company becomes too large, and then the share is grown organically, it is hard for competition authorities to stop you other than by stopping you using your company to build/support adjacencies.

Being the best
This is much broader than being the biggest. But in high scale, mature, price sensitive segments, this will likely also include being the biggest.

Low cost or high service
This assumes that you cannot have both, and it does not make sense to do some attributes on the cheap and offer others with high service.
Ryanair takes the low cost version to the extreme: the basics are cheap but you need to pay for every extra.

Cost leadership or differentiation or focus
This is a more subtle version developed by Porter (https://en.wikipedia.org/wiki/Porter's_generic_strategies).
It assumes that you cannot be the cheapest and serve different (sub) segments equally well.

Time-based competition
Coined by George Stalk (https://hbr.org/1988/07/time-the-next-source-of-competitive-advantage). Design for speed in all business processes (e.g. be the first to market to get the first mover advantage) but also in processes (such as first time right) because it will also reduce costs and improve quality.

Most innovative company
This assumes it is all about new products/services.

7.4. Incorporate the stakeholders' perspectives

Most strategies will not work if the main stakeholders are not on board. Check which are critical, such as customers, employees, shareholders, (co-)suppliers, competitors, management, unions, general public, regulators and government.
For some companies, strategy is 80% stakeholder management. In any case, decide when and how to involve the stakeholders. Generally, involving them early feels risky but makes for a more effective strategy. For high impact stakeholder issues, at least understand their issues really well right from the start. Find out what they object to and what they want in order to understand where there is optimal common ground. Doing this right requires a manual in itself.

8   Required changes of the business model

Example case:

A company acquired another company with a complementary product range in the same market segment. The acquired company only sold the product into a small number of countries and the whole idea was that the acquiring company would easily sell this product to all major countries. But there was limited competitive advantage versus existing suppliers and the R&D department was not equipped to deal with the inflow of requests from the enthusiastic sales people to adapt the product to their customer needs. The first snag is related to not understanding customer needs/competitive advantage. The second snag is about not having translated the acquisition to the required adaptation of all of the main activities (in this case, R&D).

8.1.   Map the required changes in the business model

A business model describes the value proposition (e.g. target segment, offering and revenue model) and the operating model (e.g. value chain, organisation model, and cost structure).

Business model

Target segment	Offering	Revenue model	
Customer/product segment as determined in 'relevant competitive advantage"	Value proposition as determined in 'relevant competitive advantage'	How can we best monetise our competitive advantages?	**Value position**
Value chain	**Organisation model**	**Cost structure**	
What do we need to do in-house to control the sources of our competitive advantage?	How to ensure our 'sources of competitive advantage' work together?	Which critical elements of the resulting cost structure should we manage well?	**Operating model**

I have only used the parts *Target segment* and *Offering,* and the activities/capabilities of the *Value chain* in the previous chapters for the core part of the relevant competitive advantage. This is to keep the focus and avoid going too quickly into business model building mode. Some people asked me if *Organisation* and other parts of the business model could be sources of competitive advantage. I think they can be, but only as a result of choosing the relevant competitive advantages laid out in the previous chapters. This is because it does not help if you are well-organised but have no sources of competitive advantage to organise; or have an idea for a revenue model to combine selling the product as well as the service, while you are actually very bad at servicing.

The problem that I have seen is that teams get so hooked up building a working, consistent business model that they forget to think about the core, which is building competitive advantage for customer needs in selected segments. However, when customer needs/competitive advantage/segment choice/value proposition are becoming clear, some critical elements of the business model need to be included into the iteration to check for a fit.

If you are not a start-up, then you need to have a map describing how the business model currently works. Then map the required changes in the business model to accommodate the value proposition and sources of competitive advantage. Feel free to use other business model maps, such as business model Canvas (https://nl.wikipedia.org/wiki/Business_Model_Canvas), as long as you avoid getting drawn into detailing the map before having done the first seven steps of the strategy.

In early iterations of the emerging relevant sustainable competitive advantage with the business model, check out at least *Revenue model* and the *Value chain*.

Revenue model
The question is what revenue model best monetises the relevant competitive advantage. For example, when GE got very good at servicing engines and designing engines for low service costs, it made sense to sell engine running-hours instead of engines.
Below is a simplified list of examples.

Type revenue model	Example	When to use	Example
'Free'	Advertising	High rich traffic, low willingness to pay	Facebook
Fixed price product	Single purchase	If the one-off product is the value proposition	Wedding ring
Variable price product	Success fee	If you have a high chance of winning	Lawyers
Full service	Pay per use	If you can do service well, and can design for lower service costs	GE aircraft engines
Subscription	Flat fee	If repetitive small purchases seen as hassle and you already have most of the business	Amazon Prime
Broker	Commission	Strength in sales and marketing, especially in network platforms	Booking.com

It is fine to look at revenue models for inspiration in looking for sources of competitive advantage but a revenue model itself is rarely a source of competitive advantage. If GE would have been bad at servicing engines, then it would not have benefited from selling engines by the hour.

Value chain
Think about the role in the value chain: what parts of the value chain do we need to do ourselves to be able to build/protect our source of competitive advantage?

The pure models are:

- If we need full end-to end control, then we are an '**Integrator**' (as the 'integrators' express delivery companies, such as UPS, who run and own the planes and trucks).
- If it is a very narrow part of the value chain, but we do this for many segments/products, then we can be a '**Layer player**' (e.g. Google in the e-commerce value chain: taking most of the profit pool in the end-to-end e-commerce value chain with a very strong position in a very narrow part of the value chain).
- If we own few of the activities but have full control of all outsourced activities, then we are an '**Orchestrator**'. Most commonly, the competitive advantage is about brand and design and these can be well protected, even when outsourcing the manufacturing (e.g. Dell and Nike).

Some mixed models are:

- **Outsourcing model**: outsourcing only for those parts of the value chain that are not core (that is: do not contain sources of competitive advantage), such as the back-office, or part of the manufacturing. Close to orchestrator but a narrower base of outsourcing.
- **Platforms**: A special case of 'orchestrator': linking fragmented supply to fragmented demand (e.g. Booking.com and Uber).

8.2. Decide how to realise these changes

Basically, you can realise these required changes by:
- Building a separate start-up (you have the freedom to start from scratch)
- M&A (this requires a separate manual)
- Building a separate unit, with linkages to the current core
- Adapting current business model by:
  - Adjusting capacity/capabilities of certain processes/roles
  - Re-engineering certain processes
  - Cost reduction (for all or part of the organisation)
  - A full transformation (several changes at the same time)
  - Continuous improvement

Example of a continuous improvement:
Some businesses inherently have a chicken and egg issue. The good thing is that this can also be turned into an advantage (virtuous circle). A friend did this as the chairman of a hockey club: better players → better results → better sponsors → better coach → better players. The trick is to find the right entry point to start the virtuous circle.

It also seems to work in building better EMBA programmes: better faculty → better content and delivery → better students → higher fees and better alumni → better brand → better faculty.

8.3. Determine how to adjust the organisation and metrics

Some strategic initiatives may require an adaptation of the organisation. Realise that reorganisations can absorb all of your energy for several years (at the expense of going after customers or building competitive advantage) and a reorganisation does not achieve any strategic goal in itself, it is just an enabler.

So, first check if smaller specific adaptations can be sufficient, such as:

- Cross functional teams/programmes
- Decision committees
- Adjustment of targets, shared targets
- (Initially) separate unit
- Two-hat roles
- Or change smaller parts of the organisation at level 2 or lower

If, however, a change in strategic direction is long overdue in the organisation, then prepare well to be able to do it fast and incorporate it into the roadmap that was described in Chapter 7, to avoid overloading the critical people.

Such a reorganisation is beyond the scope of this strategy manual.

8.4. Build the new culture into the new values, organisation, processes, and metrics

This is not about a few town hall meetings. It requires clearly defining what culture change you want to achieve and what hardwiring elements of the organisation will enforce this. If you want to change the company culture from being risk-averse and process-driven to being entrepreneurial and customer-driven, then you need (at least) to empower a customer experience team, and communicate about successful and unsuccessful risks taken.

8.5. Adapt your design to retain/enhance workforce engagement

Whatever metrics are used, it is very hard to catch exactly the right performance that you would like from the employees in a few metrics. So, check if the strategy, business model, and organisational set-up maintain or enhance work force engagement. This is not just about being nice to them but about engineering a fundamental match between what the company provides to the employee (targets and rewards, decision rights, training and communication), on the one hand, and the employee needs, capabilities, and beliefs, on the other hand. This topic is too big to deal with in detail in this strategy manual.

8.6. Take care of the enablers

If we have properly checked the required changes in the business model, then we should not have forgotten anything. But often we have insufficiently realised that certain support functions need to be adapted. The most common underrated changes are in the IT/digital field.

The second most common underrated change support is in HR, but this is to support the migration to the new state.
I often stress that you need to design two things (including organisation, metrics, etc.):
*   The new strategy/business model, as we have described in this chapter.
*   How to get there? If the changes are large, then often the design of getting there is more complex than the design of the new end state. The design of the migration is very briefly described in Chapter 10.

8.7. Ensure to cash in on the benefits

Sometimes the changes in the business model take so much effort that the original idea about why we were doing this gets forgotten. Make sure that the benefits of the competitive advantage you are building get to the customers and that you benefit by higher growth/profits/share. It helps to appoint someone to monitor this, before operationalising the strategy.

9 Value creation

9.1. Include a base case

To understand the impact of the strategy, you need a base case (in profit terms) to account for autonomous downward or upward market trends. I have seen situations where the business manager who was growing with the market got more credit than the person who was declining much slower than the market, where maintaining profitability in a declining market is a bigger achievement than growing with the market.

Sometimes people build a base case and a momentum case, and then overlay their strategy (option). The momentum case serves to show what happens if we execute our current plans, which becomes the baseline for the new strategy.

Sometimes the base case or momentum case will show such bad results that it serves as a case for change. In that situation, it is better to build it at the start of the project.

Typical base case

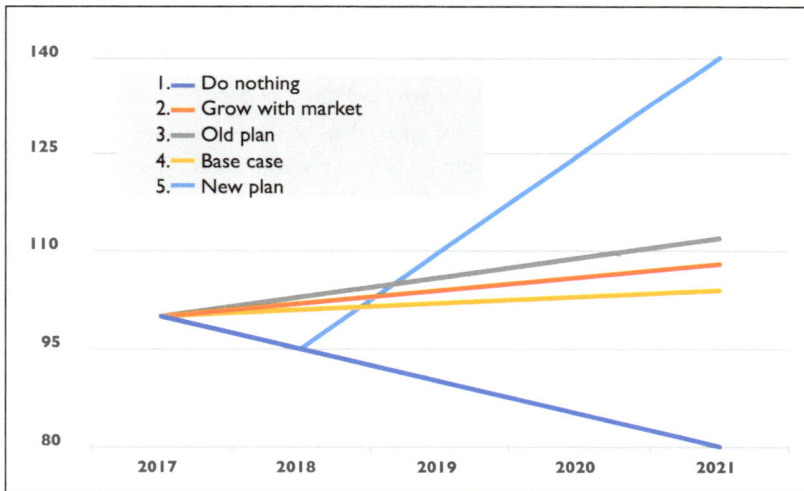

1. ■ **Do nothing:** would erode profits due to competition

2. ■ **Grow with the market** (sometimes called momentum case): includes plans to keep up with the competition

3. ■ **Old plan:** includes activities to keep a little ahead of the competition

4. ■ **Base case:** the old plan, but realising the impact was overestimated

5. ■ **New plan:** includes additional activities to win

Avoid two traps:

- Double counting of the upside with respect to base case plan
- Double counting of available resources

9.2.　Quantify the impact of the strategy

Always quantify the impact of the strategy, including both the increase in revenues and the running/investment costs. You may need to do some of this work as part of earlier iterations to choose between various strategic options (where and how to play), and should certainly keep this analysis running during the design and migration planning (Chapter 10), as often many unpleasant surprises emerge that require more (costly) adaptation.

Also do this for non-profit companies, quantifying the impact in terms of the mission; for instance, the number of adequate affordable houses at the lowest cost for a housing corporation.

If it is hard, ask yourself if the strategy (and mission) is concrete enough. Don't worry about the precise figures, keeping in mind the following two objectives for the quantification:

- It helps to find the drivers of value creation and the main uncertainties; often it helps to do this very early on and let the analysis run in parallel with the strategy project.
- Eventually, you will need a business case for decision making, either in the strategy phase or in subsequent investment decisions or operational plan.

9.3.　Determine financing needs

Some strategies require investments above the current available funds, so (new) financing is needed.

There are many forms, depending on the phase of the company (each with its own specialisation in the risk/return spectrum):

- Seed capital from founders, angel investors, accelerators, crowdfunding, subsidies
- Venture capital
- Public/private equity and loans

9.4. Conduct risk analysis

It would look more elegant to describe the risk analysis as part of Chapter 7 (*Resulting strategy*), but it is important to include the risks from building/adjusting the business model, so it is described here:

List the risks/uncertainties
- Check all assumptions
- Ask various critical internal and external people

Estimate the
- Chance of it happening
- Impact (positive and negative)

Devise mitigating actions
- High impact and high chance: → Adapt the strategy
- High impact and low chance: → Map out options versus scenarios
- Medium impact and High chance: → Add mitigating actions and incorporate total impact in value creation
- Medium impact and Low chance: → List mitigating actions

Adjust risk analysis during
- The design
- Migration planning phase

10 Design and migration plan

If you have done everything as described in Chapters 1-9, then you should have:

- A (new) vision, mission, strategy, a roadmap sequencing the main steps, and supporting stakeholders (as per Chapter 7).
- A high-level design of the required business model and organisation/metrics, also securing the right culture and workforce engagement (as per Chapter 8).
- A clear view of the value this will create (as per Chapter 9).

But this is only the high-level design, we are not ready for implementation. A lot more design work is necessary before we can implement anything.
The design and migration plan depends on the type of change required:

- A start-up
- A few tweaks, additions to an existing solid strategy
- A major change in direction
- A full transformation (requiring significant changes in many dimensions of the business model)

I don't want to incorporate a manual on change/transformation management into this strategy manual (this requires a separate manual), so instead I briefly list the main activities left to do before we can start to implement.

10.1. Adjust the team, add programme management and arrange proper mandate

Realise that the strategy team is rarely equipped or credible for operationalising the strategy, so involve the best line managers to operationalise the strategy. For larger changes, the number of teams involved usually becomes quite large. Therefore, add a programme management team of the most experienced people who can see milestones being missed well before they do so, and can orchestrate corrective action.

Ensure that all of the teams have a proper mandate:

- Clear direction
- A well-positioned mandate provider
- A well-positioned mandate taker
- Enough power over resources
- Open communication between the mandate provider and taker

"What are you still doing here? I told you what to do, go and do it!"

Taken from *The Mandate*, How good people suffer from bad mandates, and what to do about it. By Bas van Heel

10.2. Build a roadmap to sequence main changes

This is not at project plan level but is a sequence of major steps to operationalise the strategy.

For start-ups, it often looks like this: pilot, launching customer (B2B)/test market (B2C), replicate, add functionality, industrialise/scale up.

For more mature companies it is often a bit more complex and there are several angles to think about when designing the roadmap:

Understand absorption capacity
- At the frontline, and middle management, not (just) the project organisation

Choose short term long versus term mix
- Short term: fix the basics, earn a licence to operate, stop the bleeding
- Long term: build the new strategy and build new culture/organisation
- In parallel or sequence (depends on the urgency of the situation)

Type of roll out
- Big bang, sequenced: risk of big bang versus complexity of sequencing roll out

Build logical sequence
- By market segment, products/services, or geographies, primary processes, or support functions
- Optimise delivering results along the way, versus fixing all preconditions and then doing the roll-out

Choose roll-out support mechanism
- Pull forward, or replication, or central support team

Sometimes, for large change in large companies, building the roadmap requires much more effort than the strategy itself because many changes are interdependent in a large legacy environment.

If you build a business around a network model (e.g. UPS, Uber, Google advertising and Booking.com), then pay special attention to how to build critical mass for both the suppliers and users: what is the minimum number of hotels that you need to have to interest tourists, and what tourist reach do you need to convince the hotels? This is not about money (reaching critical mass to turn a profit) but much more about needing to show a positive experience to both sides, very soon after the supplier and the user have signed on. This requires smart segmentation/road mapping.

10.3. Design processes and organisation, and run pilots

For all of the changes in the business model, take the high-level design, do the design, and conduct pilots (i.e. fail fast). Although some people say that this is old-school thinking, if you want to make your strategy work in your existing company (versus starting a separate venture), then you have to follow the standard sequence of: strategy, high-level design, design and pilot, design the change roadmap and implement.
So what about agile organisations? Building them requires the same steps. Once you have succeeded, you will be agile for product development, for example, but not necessarily for the next strategic change (e.g. if your business model is becoming obsolete). Depending on the absorption capacity, you can make several changes in parallel. This is where the roadmap/sequencing discussion comes in, as discussed in the strategy chapter.

10.4. Design the migration

Also design the migration by taking the roadmap and detailing it. Note that designing the migration often takes more work than designing the new steady state.

10.5. Communicate and listen

Start communicating soon. People will know that something is happening anyway. Align the messaging with the phases of change management, and the progress of the strategy/design team: sense of urgency, the new vision/strategy, how you will make it happen.
Even more important — listen. Check if you have the right to progress to the next phase: do we understand we need to change? Do we understand/accept the new direction? Do we understand how to get there? Do we understand our new role?

10.6. Check the change (process) management

Often this important aspect (the process side of change) is assigned to a separate project team (or member) and ends up being disconnected from the programme. In my experience, the trick is the balance between the content and the process. Most change programme leadership is either content or process biased. I think content and process are equally important and need to be integrated and led by the same team.
Although some of these change elements have already been mentioned in this manual, they have not been elaborated. The best check list and clear explanation of how to lead change that I know of is *Leading Change* by John Kotter.

10.7. Build a people transition plan

A new strategic direction will have people impact, so build a solid people transition plan:

Analyse supply and demand mismatch
- Segment skill-pool
- Translate strategy to long-term requirements per skill-pool
- Map base case of available workforce per skill-pool
- Compare to find surplus/shortage per year
- Translate to required recruitment, in- and external redeployment

Recruit
- Recruit experienced people from the market
- Recruit fresh, deploy years earlier to train

Redeploy internally
- Check best match
- Retrain

Redeploy externally
- Determine external opportunities
- Offer training
- Determine minimum required transition incentive

10.8. Design and build an implementation support team

Decide on the roll-out model: pull forward, replication, central support team; size the required support team, recruit and train them. This sometimes requires so many people that recruiting and training them requires more time than anticipated. Check the capabilities and capacity of your support functions (especially HR). Add capacity for unforeseen challenges (flying squad).

F How to run a strategy project (process)

We have concentrated above on the *What*, so here we briefly deal with the *When*, *Who*, *How* and *How long*.

When

There are several moments to start a strategy project, such as:
- When a new mission is formulated
- When the feedback loop from the previous strategy needs updating
- If a pre-set trigger is pulled in an option/scenario strategy
- If signals from your continuous market/trend/customer/competitor monitors indicate that it is necessary
- The regular strategy update (if you get there)

Who

Right senior team
The strategy needs to be driven by the senior team. Sometimes the current senior team is the reason for the need for a new strategy. The supervisory board needs to find a new CEO/senior team.

Role of the strategy department/team
In an EMBA session, someone asked why their company strategy team was not so visible. Coincidentally, someone from that team was in the same EMBA class and was able to provide an answer: the strategy team (or fixed department, as in larger companies) may not be visible to everyone because their role is advisory, communication will be mostly done by the board, and their role will decrease over the course of the strategy process (diagnosis, strategy, design, migration planning and implementation).

Start with a balanced small team
Start with a small team and add capabilities according to where you need them. Ensure the right balance of power between various functions. If you have five strong people from operations, one from sales who has time, and one junior from strategy, then you may not get a competitive advantage/customer needs-based strategy.

Multifunctional teams
As mentioned in the introduction, the intended target group for this manual are

people with around ten years of experience who do an EMBA. Most are on a journey to get broader responsibilities than the function in which they have risen. Leading/ working in cross-functional teams requires different skills than in a function, such as:

- Working across a complex (matrix) organisation versus a clear single line responsibility
- Compromising to get the best for the company, not the function
- Shifting from managing to leading
- Reflection on one's own personal effectiveness (in teams)
- Understanding and coping with different types of personality
- Communicating at all 4 levels (content, procedure, relationship, emotion), using IQ and EQ
- Knowing yourself

Top down and bottom up
I have seen long debates on doing a strategy project from the top down or from the bottom up. I think that you need both bottom up (to connect with the reality on the coalface) and top down (to link to stakeholders, and the mission). It does not really matter where to start as long as the strategy process starts with questions rather than with a pre-set direction and allows several iterations. If you draw the process over time, then you end up with an 'M' shape (starting bottom up) or a 'W' shape (starting top down).

How

Use a classic problemsolving appoach (analytical framework)
Given that a strategy is about visiting all angles/functions, it inevitably risks boiling the ocean. So at the start, formulate one or two main strategic questions (e.g. 1 — "Should we diversify or not" and 2 — "If so, where and how").

Then elaborate these main questions into: subquestions, required depth, several analyses, and source. You can find the example in the Appendix, *Format 4.*

Every now and then, collect the answers on the subquestions (based on the analyses) and see if you can answer the main question. This will trigger new ideas and new questions. So, without moving off topic, adjust the table so that the whole team can see what is going on.
Some people prefer a hypothesis framework versus a questions framework. It works in the same way, and is useful if there is a reasonable idea about the outcome. Make sure to look for facts that could counter the hypotheses rather than just collect satisfying confirmation facts.

Not linear but iterative: the creative process
Again, because all elements are or should be interdependent, a strategy process cannot be a linear process that checks each question. The question framework benefits from iterations to avoid spending too much time on things that become clear early on. First, iterate mostly on the core: customer segment focus, customer needs, competitive advantage, and value proposition. Later, shift the iteration towards the *strategy and business model*, and then to *design and migration plan*. The easiest way to do this is to create an iteration heartbeat around the team meetings: force everybody to provide an update of all of their main elements.

Explicitly allow for a process that is divergent at the beginning (allow new questions and ideas, downplay questions on logic and structure) and which changes to convergent in time to have concrete output at the end. In the divergent phase, include both creative (brainstorming, asking outsiders) and analytical work in the process. Avoid mixing the two at the same moment in the same team/meeting.

How long does it take

For the core of the strategy (elements 1-9, excluding element 10: design and migration planning) if you have a good full-time team and access to customers/data, then it should take:
- One week: a high level idea for a start-up
- Six to ten weeks: a reasonable strategy for any business

Some people have asked how this works for midsized companies that do not have a strategy team. I think that it can be done equally well by fielding people from the business, as long as they spend more than 50% of their time on the project. The highly iterative character of strategy formation requires a minimum amount of dedicated time to make the team effective. Many people (from midsized companies) fall into the trap of doing many projects in parallel with all critical people participating half a day a week. Doing these projects with (at least 50%) dedicated people will significantly increase output quantity and quality with the same input time.

For decision-making, design, migration planning and implementation:
If you have a good full time team, and a strong mandate, then it will take:
- A few months: for a small change, in a small, well organised company.
- A few years: for a fundamental change, in a large, traditional company.

G Typical pitfalls and how to deal with them

There are many pitfalls when applying this simple approach but not more than in any strategy project.
I list a few here and I will detail how they can possibly be resolved:

Not realising that you need a (new) strategy
Make sure to listen to enough people in/outside your business to pick up signals that something in the market is changing or something in your company is not changing fast enough.

Thinking inside-out/group think
The risk is not getting out of the current thinking or getting stuck too quickly on one strategic option. Once you have realised this, then you have nearly solved the problem. Involve outsiders (supervisory/advisory board, external experts) to get you out of your comfort zone, and organise the strategy process to zoom-in (to really understand a critical thing) and zoom-out regularly (to avoid getting stuck on detail and to one option).

Unwillingness to accept unpleasant facts/insights
It is unusual to find a major problem that has not been thought about before. The strategy project is more likely the result of someone's uneasy feeling that something is wrong. So the fact that this project exists means that at least a few people want to know. The project needs to find sufficient proof to convince all of the other people. If the project does find new unpleasant facts, then get solid proof and find the right sequence of people to share them with.

Stuck in daily routines
It is hard to do a little bit of strategy every day. Ideally, build a team with a few people working on this full time for one or two months. If that is not available, then at the very least ensure that the lead persons have the strategy project as their priority.

No access to customers
If you start by thinking:"Let's first collect what we have, without bothering our customers", then it would be better not start at all. Even if the reason for a new strategy is not directly related to the customer (e.g. a new technology, or an aggressive competitor), a new strategy without (re-)investigating the customer is risky.

Lack of resources, unwilling to invest in fact finding
It is possible to create a strategy with limited fact finding, as long as the customer needs are solid and all of the other elements are okay on a logic level. However, not going a bit deeper risks missing an opportunity and if the resulting change is material, then you may still need to build an indisputable fact base to convince people.

Lack of a dedicated team

A fragmented team (half a day a week each) will not arrive at any insights. When short of resources, it is better to organise everyone to participate 50% for six weeks, rather than half a day for a year.

Lack of capabilities

Although you may not have a person to do all of this, you may be able to build a small team with complementary skills. If they follow the logic of this manual, then they should get quite far. Otherwise, you may need to hire some outside help.

Complexity

If you are overwhelmed by the many check-items in this manual, then just take the key example formats at the end of this manual and start to play around with them for your business. When you get stuck or are ready for the next step, you can then refer to this manual.

How to use this manual

This manual can be used in many different settings, such as:

- In a company
- Teaching/training on the job
- Consulting
- Coaching/mentoring

In a company

For an existing strategy: before you start, make sure you have a mandate to do this because if you don't, then you may upset the people you are dependent on. Use the check list to determine which elements could be underdeveloped. Initially, do this based on your own perception. Then ask a few people to do the same and compare notes. Conduct interviews for the elements that are/may be underdeveloped to find out if/why they are underdeveloped. You can then start a project to fix the gaps.

For a new strategy: in principle you will need to take care of all of the elements in this manual. But check which ones require more or less attention. This mix is always different for each strategy.

Teaching/training on the job

Preparation:

- Ask the participants to choose an existing strategy from their company; make sure they know the content of the strategy. Ideally use a strategy they are (partly) responsible for.
- Make sure that the senior management in the company is comfortable that they are doing this.
- Read this manual.
- Apply the check list at element and, even better, at underlying factor levels.

Round 1: Elements of a good strategy

- Collect the scoring on the check list and share/discuss the result in a plenary meeting.
- Briefly discuss the most common underdeveloped elements/factors.
- Breakouts in small groups (of two or three).
  - Each should prepare how to resolve weaknesses and determine barriers for doing this.
  - Discuss how to resolve the weaknesses.
- Plenary meeting: share the learning from two or three groups.

Round 2: Deep-dive(s): e.g. customer needs/competitive advantage

- Introduction (plenary): customer needs/competitive advantage.
- Breakouts in small groups (of two or three)
  - ○ Each to complete one 'customer needs/competitive advantage overview' for a given product/market combination.
  - ○ If you have time, also complete the *source of competitive advantage sheet*.
  - ○ Discuss how to do it properly (for all relevant segments).
- Plenary meeting: share learnings from two or three groups.

Round 3: Plan what to do back at work

- Introduction (plenary): options for what to do.
- Each writes a brief action plan (stay in class).
- Plenary share/discuss the result.

Consulting
Most likely, as a consultant you would not need this manual.
If you think it can help, use it in the same way as described under *In a company* and clarify the roles (who does what) with your client.

Coaching/mentoring
Ask the mentee to apply the check list in the same way as described for *In a company*. Then teach/help him/her to locate the gaps and how to fix them. If you are a former consultant taking this role: make sure that you fight the urge to do (parts of) it for your mentee.

Appendix: Four formats to get you started ⇨

Format 1: Assessment checklist for elements and underlying factors

For each element and underlying factor, assess to what extent it has been done. For clarification of the elements and factors, refer back to the corresponding chapter.

Elements and underlying factors of a good strategy	Done well	Good enough	Not good enough	Not done
1. Link to Mission				
1.1 Ensure that you have a good mission to drive your strategy				
1.2 Ensure the strategy will be the link between the mission and operational planning				
1.3 Chose an appropriate ambition level				
2. Future market context				
2.1 Take a future perspective to avoid fighting the last war				
2.2 Understand the impact of trends				
2.3 Build options against scenario's to manage uncertainty				
3. Focus product/customer segment				
3.1 Creatively define customer segments based on common needs				
3.2 Define product segment, and the corresponding market/product segment matrix				
3.3 Determine market/product segment attractiveness				
4. Key customer needs				
4.1 Define the customer DMU (incl. indirect DMU)				
4.2 Define and prioritise customer needs (incl. implicit/unmet)				
5. Value proposition				
5.1 Creatively build the proposition				
5.2 Determine customer value (what it does for the customer)				
5.3 Link proposition to business model				
5.4 Define the product				

6. Competitive advantage				
6.1 Define (potential) competitors				
6.2 Score your current/target performance versus competitors on customer needs				
6.3 List current and selected potential new sources of competitive advantage				
6.4 Understand the economics of sources of advantage				
6.5 Check (again) competitive advantage versus customer needs				
7. Resulting strategy				
7.1 Decide where to play				
7.2 Summarise how to play				
7.3 Translate into coherent strategy				
7.4 Incorporate stakeholders' perspective				
8. Required business model				
8.1 Map the required changes in business model				
8.2 Decide how to realise these changes				
8.3 Determine how to adjust the organisation and metrics				
8.4 Build the new culture into new values, organisation, processes and metrics				
8.5 Adapt design to retain/enhance workforce engagement				
8.6 Take care of the enablers				
8.7 Ensure to cash in on the benefits				
9. Value creation				
9.1 Include a base case				
9.2 Quantify the impact of the strategy				
9.3 Determine financing needs				
9.4 Conduct a risk analysis				
10. Effective plan				
10.1 Adjust the team, add programme management and arrange the proper mandate				
10.2 Build a roadmap to sequence main changes				
10.3 Design processes and organisation, and run pilots				
10.4 Design the migration				
10.5 Communicate and listen				
10.6 Check the change (process) management				
10.7 Build a people transition plan				
10.8 Design and build implementation support team				

Format 2: Customer needs versus competitive advantage

Objective:

Summary of the core of the strategy, good to start iterating from.
Map out how your company performs against the competition based on key customer needs.

Approach:

- Decide and describe which focus customer/product segment you score this for.
- List the critical customer needs for that segment.
- List the names of your four main competitors.
- Score how your competitors perform on these needs (not today, but by the time your strategy will be implemented).
- Score how you currently perform on these needs (leave blank for a start-up)
- Score how your strategy will perform on these needs.
- Describe the current source of competitive advantage that supports the score on that need (use the format on the next page for support, and list main advantages linked to each customer need).
- Describe the source of competitive advantage that you want to add based on your strategy.

For all scorings: just score the L(ow) and H(igh)

Focus customer segment:	
Focus product segment:	

Customer need		Competitor future success				Your company		Sources	
Priority	Need	Competitor 1	Competitor 2	Competitor 3	Competitor 4	Current	Strategy	Source of your competitive advantage: Current	Source of your competitive advantage: New/Strategy
1									
2									
3									
4									
5									
6									

Format 3:   Sources of competitive advantage

Objective:

Map the current and potential new sources of competitive advantage. The main sources should be summarised into the format on the previous page.
For each part of the value chain, assess to what extent scale/share or the various types of capability are an advantage, including the related impact on that part of the value chain.

Approach:

- Score each cell for your current position (check each source of competitive advantage for each of the value chain).
- Score improvements based on your strategy by adding an arrow and the new score: e.g. L→ H.
- Score impact of source of competitive advantage: current situation.
- Score impact of improvement of competitive advantage based on your strategy by adding an arrow and the new score: e.g. L → H.
- Describe how you will build each additional source of advantage.

For all scorings: just score the L(ow) and H(igh).

Part of the value chain	Share/Scale	Process	People	Culture/ Organisation	Products/IP/Techno-logy/critical assets	Digital /IT	Capital	Quality	Low cost	Speed	Describe how to build new source of competitive advantage
	Source of competitive advantage					Impact					Description
Innovation, R&D											
M&A, Alliances											
Marketing											
Sales & channels											
Customer service											
Sourcing											
Production											
Distribution											

Format 4: Classic problemsolving appoach (analytical framework)

In this table check for the following:
- Does the client agree to the main question?
- Will the answers of subquestions answer the main question?
- Where we have them, do we use hypotheses to allow focus of the analyses?
- Have we optimised the scope & priorities & depth so it is all doable, and delivers value?
- Have we checked frameworks (e.g. from our EMBA) to populate the best sub questions? (NB this problem solving approach is generic, not topic specific)
- Will the outcome of the analyses answer the subquestion?
- Are sources available, or do we need to find more simple proxies?
- Are the assigned people capable to conduct the analyses?
- Does the timeline of the analyses allow for iteration/integration of the overall results?

Main question: . . . .

Subquestion (incl hypotheses)	Depth	Analysis	Source	Who	When
Q1		1			
		2			
Q2		1			
		2			
		3			
		4			
		5			
Q3		1			
		2			
Q4		1			
		2			
		3			
Q5		1			
		2			
		3			
Q6		1			
		2			
		3			
		4			
Q7		1			
		2			
		3			
		4			

www.ingramcontent.com/pod-product-compliance
Lightning Source LLC
Chambersburg PA
CBHW041713200326
41519CB00001B/148